Title: "The HaloHabitat Manifesto"
Author: Elias Peres
First Edition
January 2014

ISBN-13: 978-1494871178

A theme-visit to

The HaloHabitat
Manifesto

with your tour-guide Elias Peres

Dedicated to my father, he was a professor in Ecology; and to my enthusiastic grandkid, he says he wants to be a Paleontologist.

The HaloHabitat Manifesto

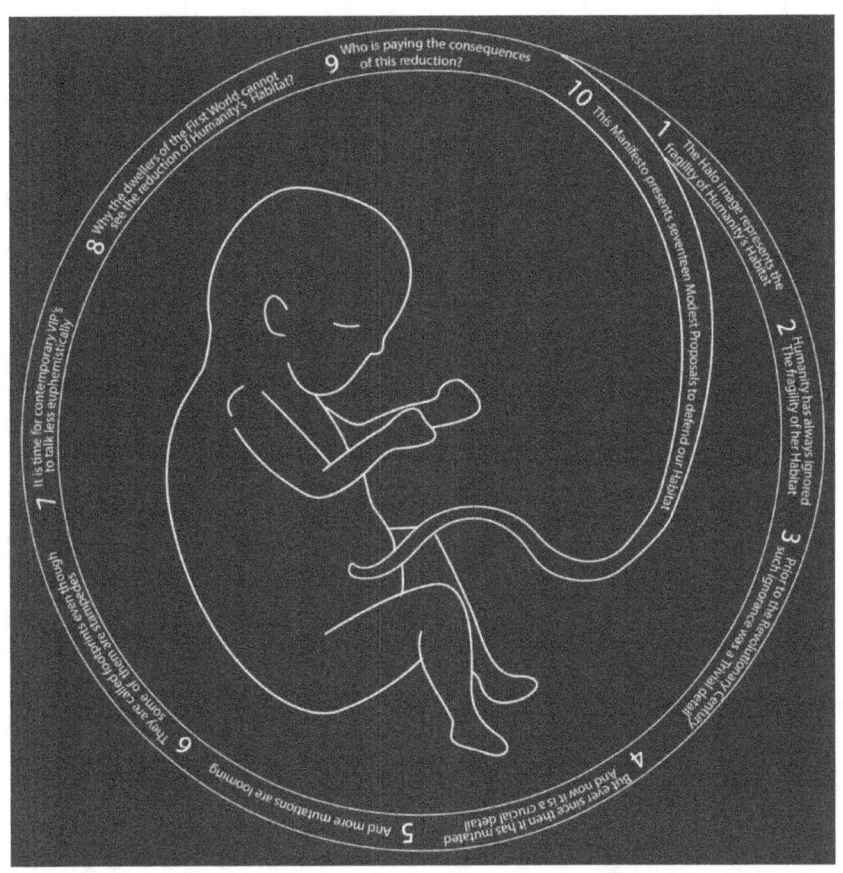

Who is paying the consequences of this reduction?

Why the dwellers of the First World cannot see the reduction of Humanity's Habitat?

The Halo image represents the fragility of Humanity's Habitat

This Manifesto presents seventeen Modest Proposals to defend our Habitat

Humanity has always ignored the fragility of her Habitat

It is time for contemporary VIP's to talk less euphemistically

Prior to the Revolutionary Century such ignorance was a Fatal detail

They are called loophins even though some of them are impostors

And more mutations are looming

But ever since then it has mutated And now it is a crucial detail

by Elias Peres

And God said to Adam: *"Be careful not to destroy My world; for if you destroy it, there is no one who will fix it after you."*
Midrash Ecclesiastes

The HaloHabitat Manifesto

1) The Halo image represents the fragility of Humanity's Habitat.
2) Humanity has always ignored the fragility of her Habitat.
3) Prior to the Revolutionary Century, such ignorance was a trivial detail.
4) But ever since then, it has mutated and now it is a crucial detail.
5) And more mutations are looming.
6) They are called footprints, even though some of them are stampedes.
7) It is time for contemporary VIPs to talk less euphemistically.
8) Why can't the dwellers of the FirstWorld see the deterioration of the HaloHabitat?
9) Who is paying the consequences of this deterioration?
10) This Manifesto presents seventeen Modest Proposals to defend our HaloHabitat.

1.-The Halo image represents the fragility of Humanity's Habitat

The HaloHabitat concept refers to an exceptional interface, which occupies a very specific location and performs very particular functions.

Such interface glows between the external face of the Crust of Planet Earth and the internal face of her Atmosphere; and one of its functions consists on hosting _VIABLE colonies_ of human beings.

I, your tour-guide for today, suggest you to imagine the HaloHabitat as a thin **coat** of fluorescent paint extended over <u>some</u> **areas** of our planet. Its thickness (3.2 miles or 5 kilometers) is less than a thousandth (0.0008) of the Earth's radius (4000 miles or 6400 kilometers).

[Thickness tip: 1000 thin coats of paint = 1 inch = 250 sheets of office paper] [1 sheet = 4 HaloHabitats]

Nowadays, when we talk about our Habitat, most of us tend to grab "versatile" terms and overlap their meanings. In order to avoid future confusions, this tour starts with a revisit of the precise meaning of some "not-so versatile" terms:

BioSphere: This is the **layer** at the periphery of Planet Earth where life can exist. There is life in the freezing poles and the implacable deserts; as well as at the ocean floors near the cauldrons where water and lava meet. [BioSphere depth: 9.6 miles or 15 kilometers ⇨ 6.4 miles below sea level; 3.2 miles above sea level].

AnthropoBioSphere: This is the **layer** <u>within</u> the BioSphere where <u>human</u> life can exist. Because this layer starts at the sea level, it completely overlaps with the lowest **stratus** of the AtmoSphere. [AnthropoBioSphere depth: 3.2 miles or 5 kms.]

AtmoSphere: This is the gaseous **layer** surrounding our planet.

AeroSphere: This is the lowest **stratus** of the AtmoSphere; its level of density of breathable air is adequate for <u>average</u> human beings. [AeroSphere depth: 3.2 miles or 5 kms. immediately above sea level].

AnthropoSphere: This is a circumferential **net** woven by Mankind's _**daily**_ influence. This **net** surrounds the Earth; it dives as deep as 6.4 miles downward (deep mining, oil drillings, the probing of the ocean abysses); and it rises hundreds, even thousands, of miles skyward (the communication satellites, the manned stations).

Land,, **Firm-Ground**, **Solid-Mass.** These names correspond to that 30% of the Earth's Surface not covered by the Liquid-Mass (the oceans and the seas).

It shall be noted that a vast area of the Firm-Ground is not feasible for agriculture or human habitation (30% of this 30% is desert).

Earth's-Surface, **Earth's-Crust**, **Earth's-Face**. These names are employed more frequently than their synonym Earth's-Skin; maybe because the former sound more resilient than the latter.

At the zenith of Mount Everest, the Earth's radius reaches almost 4035 miles. From its center to its surface, our planet presents four concentric **layers**: the Inner Core (800 miles thick), the Outer Core (1400 miles thick), the Mantle (1800 miles thick), and the LithoSphere (up to 35 miles thick).

The term LithoSphere means "rocky-sphere" and it refers to a **layer** of brittle rock; the lower stratus of this **layer** interacts with the Mantle, while its upper stratus becomes... the Crust!

The Crust is mostly made of basalt; this basic rock builds the floor of the oceans and the basement of the continents. The continents are aggregates of granitic rock, which is lighter than basalt.

The cooled and solidified LithoSphere floats atop the hot and viscous Mantle; but this ride takes a toll: the LithoSphere is incessantly reconfigured.

(Hence the origin of tectonic plates, fissures, earthquakes, tsunamis, fossils of creatures from ancient seas found on the slopes of modern mountains, oil deposits, plateaus that once were at the bottom of the seas and now are fertile highlands).

Terrestrial Globe: The equatorial circumference of Planet Earth is 24901 miles (40075 kilometers); at the usual walking speed -3.2 mph or 5 kph - it would take 8000 hours for an excursionist to cover that distance. On the other hand, it only takes one hour to stroll for a distance equal to the depth of the HaloHabitat.

4

2.-Humanity has always ignored the fragility or her Habitat

As of this year 2014, 7.5 billion human beings populate Planet Earth; from among them, it is estimated that 2.5 billion <u>believe</u> there is global-warming, 2.5 billion <u>deny</u> there is global-warming, and 2.5 billion <u>are too busy</u> to participate in this debate.   [100÷3=33.33]

Secondly, from among those who believe there is global-warming: A third of them point to the impact caused by human beings. Another third blame other major factors. And the last third remain undecided. [33.33÷3=11.11]

Thirdly, from among those who implicate mankind: A third of them (the Activists) are convinced mankind can reverse global-warming. Another third (the Fatalists) believe there is nothing we can do to revert it. And the last third (the Opportunists) expect to take advantage of this situation. As a matter of fact, many Opportunists have become Deniers of global-warming; how come? They have realized that <u>such denial is good for business</u> (like selling bungalows in flood prone areas), and/or <u>keeps them in power</u> (politicians and tycoons are keenly aware that many voters and investors are sincere Deniers).   [11.11÷3=3.70]

Finally, from among the Activists: A third of them (the ProActivists) claim global-warming is a grave and urgent issue. Another third (the RetroActivists) affirm this matter is serious but not urgent. And the last third (the DeActivated) have chosen to trust those lobbyists who reassure global-warming is neither grave nor urgent and, in any event, the bureaucrats and the technologists will know how to manage it. [3.70÷3=1.23]

Now, isn't this amazing? Only one percent of contemporary human beings are **ALREADY** seeing global-warming as an urgent and potentially lethal condition?

Well, that small percentage of ProActivists (I include myself among them) shouldn't be a surprise. How can we expect to gain more sympathizers when we ourselves are undermining our case?

This sounds ironic, "undermining our own case"? .....How?

We do so when we employ the "global-warming" headline. Maybe this is an appropriate time to admit that our pioneers chose a blunt characterization of Ms. HaloHabitat (she is not a globe, <u>she is an interface</u>), and presented an easy to discredit claim ("warming" can be attributed to numerous and very diverse factors; and some of them can neutralize each other).

Such an inadequate headline has prompted several of our fellow ProActivists to present a substitute, "climate-change"; but there is a problem: This substitution has produced an unintended outcome; it made the Deniers' job easier! And they jumped on the occasion! Let's listen to some comments from two lucky Deniers.

First, from a global-warming Denier:

When you Warmers declare "global" and you mean the Earthly Globe, you must keep three details in mind: a) On the planetary scale, the Earth is a robust twentysomething; she is only 4.5 billion years old! b) She has the best and most fruitful **eons** of her life ahead of her. c) The Earth's inner core temperature is the same as the temperature at the Sun's surface, so ....pleaase! ....don't come to me worrying about "warming"!

Now, if you are referring to the BioSphere; what component of it concerns you the most? The air, the land, the water? The other life-forms sharing the BioSphere with the human species? Have you heard about Pinatubo and Krakatoa? Did you know that the Yellowstone Caldera is past due for a big eruption? A hearty burp of ash from a super-volcano can affect the whole BioSphere, by altering the AtmoSphere and reflecting the sunlight. Then you Warmers will have to deal with Global-Freezing!!

Next, from a climate-change Denier:

Geez Warmers!!... What part of "all-over-the-place" you don't get? If "global-warming" sounds vague, "climate-change" sounds even vaguer. ...Hmm, I shouldn't alert you guys about this, but ...didn't you notice that "global-warming" conveys some sense of urgency while "climate-change" doesn't?

You Warmers got to be specific; don't forget that The Earth has gone and will go thru countless and diverse climate-changes: daily, seasonal, cyclical, glacial, local, micro, macro, damaging, beneficial....

3.-Prior to the Eighteen Century such ignorance was a trivial detail

While listening to our Deniers friends, did you realize that they and the Warmers display similar ignorance about our Habitat? All of them associate our Habitat with robust shapes like globes and spheres, or with vague images like climate and environment; but they avoid delicate and precise characterizations.

Is such "ignorance" sincere? A sample of this term's first meaning: Not knowing?

Or is it pretended? A sample of its second meaning: Not paying attention, eluding, rejecting?

And the answer to these questions is: Both scenarios are valid.

Human beings have always **ignored** the fragility of their Habitat: If in the olden times virtually everybody **ignored** (didn't know about) such fragility; nowadays almost everybody **ignores** (doesn't pay attention to) her.

But such a discourtesy must not keep going on, for it is placing the very survival of our species at risk.

Therefore, Humanity needs a critical-mass of human beings willing to perform two important missions: a) Acknowledge the fragility of our Habitat. b) Team work with such limitation.

Prior to the Eighteenth Century, for human beings to decide if our Habitat was a robust sphere or a fragile interface, would have been a disconcerting and useless exercise.

Back then, most human beings had not yet completed the transition from believing their Habitat was an immense platform (sturdy Mr. FlatWorld) into accepting it was more like a sphere (sturdier Mr. GlobeHabitat).

And, from the BioSphere's perspective, Humanity was easily tolerable, almost irrelevant.

It is true that the diverse human **peoples** had **already** demonstrated to be peculiarly chaotic (both between themselves as well as within themselves); but the scraps produced by their ***Basic Activities of Daily***

Living (BADLys) were easy to keep under control (natural degradation recycled them within months if not weeks).

Furthermore, instinctively, **_human beings preferred to keep themselves within their specific habitat_** (the AnthropoBioSphere, that sublayer within the BioSphere where human life can exist).

Just venturing outside of that sublayer meant ---even our most audacious explorers admitted so--- risking to be eliminated from the face of the Earth and from The Book of History.

The fact that human beings had domesticated diverse plants and animals; caused the extinction of some species (like the urus and the dodos); and erected many impressive buildings, was still manageable for the BioSphere, whose threshold for Humanity is: **"As long as _humans dwell within their SpecificHabitat, and the debris of their BADLys is naturally recyclable, they are tolerable."_**

SpecificHabitat? **Yes indeed!** If we human beings are really serious about preserving, protecting and defending our present Habitat, we got to be specific.
So far, this Halo is the sole Habitat we have access to.

It is pleasant and enlightening to engage in some generalizations, and theorize about lots of extraterrestrial habitats waiting to be discovered and colonized. Present human beings have already coined names for the specific habitats of _future-and-improved_ human peoples: **WaterWorld** (for the Aquatics, those humans able to breathe water); **MarsHaloHabitat** (in Mars, not to be confused with the Earth's GeoHaloHabitat); **SeleneDomes** (colonies on the surface of our Moon); **GanymedePolyps** (deep in that saltwater-ocean 150 miles below the frozen surface of Jupiter's largest moon); **BionicsNirvana** (the nano-implants will make the superhumans the norm rather than the exception); **Pie-in-the-sky-MotherShips** (waiting to be occupied by ship jumpers); **UNlimited-UNregulated-parking** (for future UNdiplomats).

Okay now! After observing these seven exponents of _far-futuristic_ proposals, I invite you to look the other way, towards the _recent-past_.....
What on Earth happened two-and-a-half centuries ago?

4.-But ever since then, it has mutated and now it is a crucial detail

For millions of years Humanity has ignored the fragility of her Habitat; which is understandable since Humanity was too busy barking at wrong trees (like Mr. FlatWorld and Mr. GlobeHabitat).

How come this ignorance has transformed from being a trivial detail into being a crucial detail?

This mutation started 250 years ago, during the last half of the Revolutionary Century, with a rapid influx of beginnings: The First Industrial Revolution (1763), The Birth of Modern Chemistry (1773), The American Revolution (1775), The Economic Thought Revolution (1776), The French Revolution (1789), The Modern Stock Exchanges (London and New York in the 1790's).

Initially, most of the changes made possible by these movements were <u>additive</u>, <u>arithmetic</u>, **<u>linear</u>**. (I suggest you to associate this stage to the progress of a fighter-jet taxiing from the hangar to the runway. Trivial detail: its canopy is raised.)

Later on, several of those changes synergized and became <u>multiplicative</u>, <u>geometric</u>, **<u>exponential</u>**. (The fighter's take-off and its almost vertical ascent. Crucial detail: its canopy is securely closed.)

This <u>routine</u> "from linear-progress to exponential-progress" is also known as "from linear-growth to exponential-growth" (the latter is the favorite of those propagandists of **<u>growth-at-all-costs</u>**; particularly the exponential-growth phase). Said propagandists fear that acknowledging the ***real and fragile*** Ms. HaloHabitat may not be good for their agendas; thus, they keep barking at the ***imaginary and robust*** Mr. GlobeHabitat.

Meanwhile, Ms. HaloHabitat is being damaged by the collateral effects of the exponential-growths. According to some experts, the brutality of the attacks inflicted upon Ms. HaloHabitat... may obligate her to write-off Humanity... as early as within the next three decades!

But other experts dismiss such forecast as alarmist, and they advise human beings to wait for further data.

Regardless of the academicians' debates, more and more lay folks want to know if some allegedly alarming growths are really exponential; they are puzzled due to all that fuss about "footprints".

Disclaimer: "footprint" is the contemporary euphemism for "threat in exponential progress". Having clarified this point, let's review some footprints; starting with seven of the most mentioned ones:

a.-**Greenhouse Footprint:** Compelled to reduce their emissions of greenhouse **gases**, numerous organizations are resorting to diverse strategies like resources-shuffling, credits-trading, and allowances-swap. Let's see how they work:

A car manufacturer can conveniently reshuffle its lineup of vehicles [gas/electric/hybrids -or- compact/medium/big]; or buy the unused allowance of another manufacturer.

Underdeveloped nations may sell their credits to developed ones, who usually pay with foreign aid.

The States can also swap allowances. The following is a dialogue between a top officer of the CARB (California Air Resources Board) and a top officer of the WARB (Wisconsin Air Resources Board):
- WARB: You Californians have to pay us more for our unused credits; after all, you have lots of high tech industries and too many cars! You got to comply with the Carbon Market Regulations!
- CARB: Calm down! You have too many cows, and they are relentless methane-emitters!
- WARB: You also have lots of cows!!
- CARB: Yup, but our cows are happy cows!

After this exchange, both officers reconciled and went to a steak house (at the taxpayers' expense).

Now, for some reason, it seems that everybody (governments, corporations, Warmers, Deniers) prefers to stay focused on the **gaseous** facet of the Carbon Footprint.

Why? Maybe because this phase carries less political risks, it is easy to spin, it seems an abstraction, it eclipses other issues and --as a Denier friend said-- since the greenhouse effect can be rendered moot by a hearty burp of a super volcano, what's the point on worrying about it?

5.-And more mutations are looming

b.-**Pavementation Footprint:** Contrary to the greenhouse effect, this footprint doesn't seem an abstraction, because we can see it and walk on it. Just let's think about the so many ever-growing cities, the widened highways, mega-parking lots, bunches of airports, factories, stadiums, houses of every type (summer, winter, for investment).

Though the Pavementation Footprint cannot be ignored, it can be optimistically presented: "It's the trade-off for progress, and its implant on fertile lands has been balanced by the Agricultural Revolution."

c.-**Inconclusive Footprint:** You might not have heard this headline previously, but you must have heard a lot about inconclusive findings. These ones are a characteristic of the bureaucratic and academic entities, and they are periodical and timid.

Let's see a recent example: The United Nations Intergovernmental Panel on Climate Change (IPCC) reported on September 2013 that *"human influence is now thought **extremely likely** to be **the dominant cause** of global warming since the mid-20th Century".*

Even though this report is still no conclusive, it is far less timid than previous IPCC findings.

We can understand the bureaucrats' and academicians' anxiety to protect their jobs and tenures, but we shall not accept their indecisiveness; the latter carries with it a major waste of precious time, fleeting resources, and the public's patience.

d.-**Independentist Footprint:** The 1776 American Independence unfurled the liberty fervor across The Americas. By 1826 Spain had lost all her Continental American colonies, and kept only a few islands on the Caribbean Sea. The Continental Americans were able to consolidate their independence thanks in part to President James Monroe's doctrine "The Americas for the Americans" (year 1823).

Nowadays, the advocates of American-Immigrants embrace the Monroe doctrine; but the detractors of American-Immigrants argue that Monroe meant "America for the Americans". Yes, you guessed it correctly! The American Congress is restudying this doctrine, but its findings have been... inconclusive.

The independentist fervor kept proliferating, and its fruits nourish the current membership of the United Nations Organization (UNO).

From 46 members in 1945, it grew to 193 in 2013, and it is expected to reach 460 by 2045. (A ten times growth! What a proper gift to celebrate the 100th Anniversary of the UNO!)

If you believe this estimate is unrealistic, you shall know that each one of the UNO members has its own potpourri of separatist districts.

Some separatists have even placed their new names in circulation: North Italy, French Speaking Canada, Texas4.1, Central Carolina, Austral Australia, Boreal Australia, Gourmet France (millions of Frenchmen are reluctant to incorporate fast food in their lifestyle).

So much independentism should prompt us to ask the UNO: Which of these two priorities takes precedence? Recruiting new members or protecting Humanity's HaloHabitat?

e.-**Bubble Footprint:** Most preschool kids know exponentiality and ephemerality. They may not have heard such words, but they do know how to make bubbles with soapy water, and how temporary these bubbles are.

In the meantime, we the adults have to deal with other kinds of bubbles and their legacies: internet bubble, housing bubble, educational bubble, stocks bubble, entitlements bubble, arrogance bubble...

f.-**Personal Footprint:** It is advisable for you to monitor your very own individual ecological impact; for this is the area where you can exert more changes. You shall always strive to minimize the many footprints you generate thru your household, belongings, plastics, lifestyle, BADLys and so on.

g.-**Genetically-managed FOOD-print:** The uppity remark *"If you need to ask for the price of this item, you cannot afford it"* has a distant cousin, the helpful *"This food has been genetically-managed, so you can afford it."*

Such handling may occur at any of the facets ---***seeds, fertilizers, pesticides, fodder, antibiotics, water treatment, hormones, packaging*** --- of the production of processed, natural... even organic foods!

6.-They are called footprints though some of them are stampedes

As we approach some of the hardly mentioned footprints, you may be wondering why such a silence; if so, consider this powerful deterrent: Merely mentioning these unmentionables can end the careers, sink the fortunes and demolish the top-status of politicians, entrepreneurs, clerics, celebrities, journalists, bureaucrats, etc..

Hence the motto *"If you want to keep your top-status, don't even think about the unmentionables."*

Dear friends: my parents raised me frugal, I love my simple lifestyle, I am just a happy go lucky tour-guide. So, since I have no top-status to keep, I guess I can afford to mention four unmentionables.

A.-**Arrogant-aristocrats Footprint:** As the revolution loomed in France, the aristocrats kept disregarding it. In perhaps the most disputed foot-in-mouth rumor, to *"The people wants bread!"* clamor, Queen Marie Antoinette replied *"Let them eat cake!"* Needless to say, this rumor exacerbated the populace's anger.

Scholars of The French Revolution praise its *"Liberty, Equality, Fraternity"* ideal; but they aren't so happy about its popular-at-all-social-levels worldwide legacy *"Eating my cake and having it too!"*

Nowadays, Humanity is carpet-bombed by the consumerism propaganda: "The customer is King. The sky is the limit. You are worth it. You are entitled to it. They owe you. It's yours for the taking. Go for it." (These are discrete samples; to see the brazen ones, type 'consumerism propaganda' in any search-engine.)

Untold events have taught us this: If virtues are overexerted, they can turn into defects: hope into procrastination, charity into enabling wrongdoers, dignity into pomposity, pride into arrogance.

It seems that the consumerism propaganda has expedited the arrival of The French Revolution's second promise, Social Equality; ...Ahem! ...A grotesque social equality, but equality nonetheless.

Humanity is now a civilization of Aristocrats. Every nation in the world is plagued by them: Arrogant pedestrians/Arrogant drivers. Arrogant elderly/Arrogant youth. Arrogant taxpayers/Arrogant welfare recipients.   Arrogant academicians/Arrogant illiterates.   Arrogant righteous/Arrogant sinners.

B.-**Unusual-obesity Footprint:** The concern caused by the growing number of obese human beings, is deepened by the unusual shapes of modern obesity. Such shapes suggest that the *air*, water and food we are ingesting contain traces of hormone-like substances.

A possible source of them? Microscopic plastic flakes. (Dusting off from containers, makeup, fabrics, pillows, cars, school supplies, toys,...)

Let's see: 16 *breaths* per minute × 1440 minutes per day × 365 days = 8.4 million *breaths* per year.

Modern obesity might just be the tip of the *Ingestive-Iceberg*; many other conditions (developmental, immunological, behavioral) may be related to the ingestion of *modern* microscopic particles.

C.-**Continents of Unbiodegradable-Refuse Sow Extinction (CURSE):** The first continent made of UBD-R has consolidated in the 'idle' center of the Pacific Ocean, a second one is converging at an 'idle' area of the Atlantic Ocean, and there are lots of islands and islets made of UBD-R.

Since the 1950's, 1.5 billion tons of plastics have been discarded; it seems that part of them are accumulated in the CURSE continents.

D.-**BADLys Footprint:** Nowadays, the **Basic-Activities-of-Daily-Living of any human** yield an amount of **UnBioDegradable-Refuse (UBD-R)**. (Have you appraised your personal BADLys footprint?)

The advent of plastic made possible the production of cheap and lightweight utensils. Since these wares are so affordable, they are massively used and massively discarded by the masses of consumers.

Let's itemize some BADLys related wares: Food wrappers, cups, plates, cutlery. Jars or sachets for soap, toothpaste, shampoos, pills. Cloths, razors, gloves, masks.

Hence a question: By the age a contemporary Average-Joe retires, what's the amount of UBD-R he has generated?

And its two answers: Weight-wise? A ton. Volume-wise? A trailer. (Besides his BADLys, Average-Joe has consumed upbringing, schooling, socializing, housing, transport, health-care, hobbies...)

7.-It is time for contemporary VIPs to talk less euphemistically

But first, and in order to be fair to the Very Important Persons, we have to admit the following: All along Humanity's existence, virtually all her VIPs have resorted to euphemisms. Furthermore; we may meet someday more advanced, non-Human cultures, and learn that their VIPs also prefer to resort to euphemisms.

Why such preference? There are numerous and compelling reasons that explain it; let's attend to four of them:

- Self-preservation. (This reason is self-explanatory.)
- Greed: Some VIPs may wonder "What's the use of me being influential if I'm not profiting from it?"
- Prudence: VIPs know that their openly frank comments can grievously harm other persons or missions.
- Patience: Sometimes even the VIPs must wait; what if the masses are not ready to hear the truth?

Thus, it seems that the burden of frank-talk rests on the shoulders of the **not-VIPs**, which means almost all of us.

We are about to visit three more stampedes; they are along the path to the last pavilion, the one where some modest proposals to protect Ms. HaloHabitat are presented.

I.-Humanity-overpopulation Footprint:

By year 1760, it had taken 2.5 million years for Humanity to attain the 750 million population level. And now, in 2014, our population is 7,500 million.

A tenfold growth in one ten thousandth of the time! A one hundred thousand exponential-growth!

(750 million people × **10** = 7.5 billion people)

(250years ÷ 2.5millionyears = **0.0001**)   (10 ÷ 0.0001 = **100,000**)

Now, if most of us, the 7.5 billion contemporary human beings, may reach retirement age; and each one of us may generate at least one ton of lightweight UBD-R: Where is this equivalent of 7.5 billion trailers of UnBioDegradable-Refuse going to end up? Is this the seed for five new CURSE continents?

II.-**Worldwide-escapism Footprint:**

Besides being ubiquitous, this escapism is erratic, zigzagging, back and forth. By foot, by boat, by plane. ThirdWorld youth migrate to the FirstWorld; FirstWorld elderly relocate in the ThirdWorld. Bored ruralites yearn for big city life; tired urbanites flee to the countryside. From domestic reality to virtual reality. Seeking relief via shopping, sensorialism and drugs. From houses to bunkers. From enjoying real food to enjoying powder delicacies (add water—stir---drink this steak).

Although most of these escapists may be harmless, some of them are definitely dangerous; especially those who despise this HaloHabitat, the sole habitat Humanity have access to.

Why is it so difficult for these latter ones to grasp the following?: Harming this HaloHabitat equals to harming innumerable human beings, both of the present and the future generations.

Have you seen some of these usual suspects?: Those that pollute Ms. HaloHabitat. Those that pontificate against her. Those ship-jumpers financing space shuttles to nowhere. Those willing to entomb themselves in plastic (have you seen their survival kits?). Those that worship technology. Those that worship bureaucracy.

III.-**Calamity-fatigue Footprint:**

In this era of information overload, billions of human beings show symptoms of "overexposure to calamitous warnings":

Millions of them seem really anxious and keep asking when will the new world arrive, why is it taking so long to manifest?

Millions are fed up; they don't want to hear any more about false alarms, astute doomsday "clearances", Habitat lectures (like this one).

Millions have become impatient Calamity-Joes searching for ways to expedite the arrival of the new world. Since some of such ways entail the annihilation of this HaloHabitat, most of these guys are fascinated with weapons of mass destruction and don't care about environmental protection.

Millions don't want to give up but they are already thinking *"Maybe the time has come for human beings to gratefully enjoy the ending chapters of this epic voyage with Ms. HaloHabitat; and to philosophically accept whatever Fate has in store for us."*

Millions are in denial.

8.-Why can't the FirstWorld's dwellers see our HaloHabitat's deterioration?

Of course they can see it! Perhaps from the distance, watching televised newscasts about far and away territories. Or perhaps up close and personal, reluctantly taking a walk in a neighborhood they usually avoid. Seeing so many newly-arrived people, hearing their exotic accents; at hospital emergency-rooms, at the school, at a new branch of an old congregation: Welcome to the Environmental-Refugees Era!

The DestinationCountries (DCs) have accepted refugees fleeing from lands where they face persecution, even death, because of their beliefs. Furthermore, depending on the cycles of the economy, the DCs have been more or less receptive of refugees fleeing from poverty. And now, the DCs are getting acquainted with a new kind of refugees, those persecuted by ecological disasters.

Pressed by their overwhelmed citizenries, the governments of the DestinationCountries are resorting to varied political tools.

Some of such policies are cold:

1) Grant foreign aid to governments of OriginCountries, provided they stop their citizens' exodus.

2) Dictate immigration laws that only consider those applicants that wait in their OriginCountries.

3) Become TransitCountries by "subtly" enticing the refugees to keep moving. A recent exhibit of this subterfuge was provided by some officers in Italy; they procured passes and bus-fare to refugees from Libya and Somalia, Italy's former colonies. (Next stops? The alternative DestinationCountries: Germany, Sweden, Norway...)

And some policies are cruel:

1) Looking the other way while NIMDISTS [Not-In-My-District] militants assault the refugees.

2) Imprisoning the refugees (this policy grants an extra benefit: it pleases the shareholders of private-prisons corporations).

3) Inflicting a perverse torture, false hope: give empty promises to refugees, and use them as pawns of political agendas.

Besides persecution in their OriginCountries, the Environmental-Refugees face death: By poisoning (contaminated waters). By famine (drought-flood cycles). By lethal fights for dwindling resources (these ones intertwine with sectarian wars and regime changes). By bigger than ever typhoons.

But, in the first place, how did these refugees become the prey of environmental persecution?

Part of this tragedy is caused by ThirdWorld habits, like: 1) Informal mining (it poisons the waters with metals and solvents). 2) Overfarming (leads to deforestation and more floods). 3) Overpopulation.

And part of it is caused by FirstWorld practices, like: 1) **Vicarious** overpopulation: In order to **discredit** the contraception **policies** of ThirdWorld nations, **proselytizing agents** from the FirstWorld move to those nations. 2) **Versatility**: Once the fish **banks** of **rich** countries show **signs** of **depletion**, the fleets of the FirstWorld **opt for** fishing in seas around **poor** countries. 3) The 1.5 **billion consumers** of the FirstWorld **sum** 20% of the world **markets**; but they **spend** 80% of the **yearly extraction** of non-renewable **resources**. 4) FirstWorld **investors** are **hoarding** water, farming and mining **assets** in the ThirdWorld. 5) When FirstWorld's **corporations** reassign **sources**, they don't always **disclose** it to the **Average**-Joes, **media** or **regulators**. 6) Then, would you blame Average-Joe for not knowing about a **discrete exchange performed** thousands of miles away?

Many terms in the previous paragraph have been remarked; this was done so we can briefly talk about **financial savvy**. This one is a skill with worldwide applicability, everyone should acquire it; not only to avoid being victimized by other civilians or the IRS, but also to thrive within the system.

The financial recession of 2008 left millions without a job; in despite of that, many Hals (**H**appy **a**nd **l**ucky guy**s**) kept on with their pricey lifestyles. How come? They "knew" they would get a job within six months; and they had savings and many credit cards. Sure enough! These Hals got better jobs promptly, and not even their next door neighbors learned about their brief unemployment. Good for them!

9.-Who is paying the consequences of this deterioration?

Now that we see the Environmental-Refugees as a manifestation of Ms. HaloHabitat deterioration, a financial question is besieging us: Who is paying the consequences of such deterioration, and how?

These ones are some tentative answers:
Maybe the poor countries with their natural resources. Or the rich nations with their foreign aid packages. Or the ThirdWorld inhabitants thru their tears and suffering. Or the FirstWorld workers contributing heavy taxes. Or those generous trillionaires implementing billionaire trusts for charitable foundations.

And this one is an integrative answer:
Each one and all of them; thru the ultimate payer, Ms. HaloHabitat. This answer adds a caveat: Do not confuse being the ultimate payer with paying the ultimate price!

We human beings have always perceived that our Habitat can exist without us. Such perception has been addressed first by religious, and later by philosophical and financial teachings. Regrettably, humans just being humans, we've conveniently twisted and stretched such teachings.

Most religions affirm that God has granted us rent-free access to this Habitat. Many faiths proclaim we are the outright owners of Planet Earth. And some creeds warn us not to become too attached to this temporary world, since the permanent and better one is about to arrive.
Whichever the case, no major religion gives us permission to damage this Habitat, regardless of it being temporary or permanent.
Any major religion has factions that dream on expediting the advent of the next world. Unfortunately, some of said factions have designed an expeditious but insane move: destroy the present world. Thus, they're stockpiling arms, building bunkers, adding no-biodegradable pollution, inciting wars, and so on.

Religion means ***again*** (RE) ***unite*** (LIGARE) with God; and philosophy means ***love of*** (PHILO) ***wisdom*** (SOPHY). Since God is Supreme Wisdom, it is hopeful to imagine religion and philosophy as the two faces of the most precious ring.

This hope supports our belief that God likes most of the artistic and scientific achievements attained by human beings (in other words, ***those achievements that don't jeopardize our Ecosystem***).

Economics means ***home*** (ECO) ***management*** (NOMICS); however, since eco resonates kind of homely, many people prefer a synonym that might not be so accurate but resonates more glamorous: finances.

Anyway, when it comes to finances, human beings resort to many methods, both the fair and the unfair. Let's observe five of the latter:

a.-False pretenses: Signing a contract without intention of fulfilling it, or holding mental reservations.

b.-Reneging of obligations: Changing your mind; breach of contract.

c.-Misappropriation of funds: Malversation, plundering.

d.-Ponzi Scheme: A connoisseur charms some investors, pays them better than average returns, this attracts new investors; all along, he rewards himself handsomely. That's it! This feast can go undetected for years, as long as new investors supply new funds.

e.-Onion Scheme: A guy obtains a loan, timely pays its monthly installments and, after several months, he renegotiates it (and for a bigger amount). Now that the lenders believe that guy is a good risk, he can keep adding new layers of credit. His credit-onion is expanding!

The beauty of the Onion Scheme is that it isn't a crime: After a merry interlude a debtor may decide he "cannot" pay his debts; then he simply cuts some loses and files for bankruptcy. That's it! His debts are the banks' and the taxpayers' problem now.

From the dawn of History, methods like the listed above have assisted the big debtors: kingdoms and nations. In those olden times small defaulters were sent to prison or labor-camps; but that doesn't happen anymore.   Not surprisingly, this modern immunity has emboldened countless Average-Joes and small merchants.

The problem with all these kinds and sizes of defaulters is that they may get addicted to declaring bankruptcy; its thrills and tax breaks are priceless. Why not resort to it when negotiating with Ms. HaloHabitat?

10.-Seventeen Modest Proposals to defend our HaloHabitat

We've just been notified that Ms. HaloHabitat is the ultimate payer, but she will not pay the ultimate price. Perhaps Ms. HaloHabitat will dissolve and take Humanity with her; or perhaps she will simply cut her losses and write-off us. She is a financially savvy lady, and she knows she has a number of options.

Hence the 1st MP:

We human beings must understand that Ms. HaloHabitat <u>can indeed</u> nix us, but we <u>cannot</u> nix Her.

2nd MP: *We must remember that out of our sight may mean out of our mind, but it doesn't mean out of our existence.*

The Oceans cover 70% of Planet Earth's surface; major changes and pollutions are converging in their "idle" and "remote" areas, but their chicks are landing and congregating in the Continents!!

3rd MP: *We must look beyond the <u>GASEOUS</u> carbon footprint* (greenhouse gases emissions).

Ironically, this smoke curtain conceals the <u>SOLID</u> carbon footprint (continents, islands and islets of discarded plastics).

4th MP: *We must look beyond the scenery of any activity, event or product; and sponsor the ones that generate less refuse*.

The trinkets and glittery of shows, the pomp and circumstance of ceremonies, the layouts at stores, the packaging of products, the fashion roulette, the hobbies, the family traditions,... any activity, event or product generates an amount of "preventable" refuse.

5th MP: *We must strive to attain a Responsible Level of Human Population (RLHP); the first step toward this goal consists on looking beyond the barrier of euphemisms.*

But where is that barrier? When people resorts to expressions like "educational rat-race", "tiger moms", "jobless post-graduates", "this is the new normal", what are they implying?   Are they alluding to overpopulation?.

6th MP: *Appeasing our Habitat shall be our top <u>pragmatic</u> priority.*

All the other pragmatic priorities of Humanity: safety, jobs, health, education, housing, peace, infrastructure........ are viable if, and only if, our Habitat is viable.

7th MP: *We must appreciate the power of synergism.*

Small deeds working together yield immense results.

And we can start right now! By minimizing our <u>individual-footprint</u>! (BADLys, lifestyle, exigencies, clutter, debris).

8th MP: *We, as individuals, must persuade our corporations to reduce their <u>corporate-footprints</u>.*

The synergism of millions of individuals reducing our <u>personal-footprints</u> might inspire our corporations (governments, committees, congregations, businesses, workplaces, neighborhoods, schools, clubs, families).

Who knows whether our individual examples will persuade our corporations? But we got to do something!!

9th MP: *We must stop irresponsible recruitment.*

Virtually, and regardless of their specialty, all proselytizers must meet certain quotas to advance their agendas.

However, and unfortunately:

- Some politicians articulate empty promises.
- Some financiers sell confusing financial products to confused customers.
- Some proselytizers, deployed to the ThirdWorld, don't really explain to the potential converts that conversion isn't a ticket for admission into the FirstWorld. Paradoxically, the staunch sponsors of such proselytizers figure (would you believe it?) among the most ruthless domestic foes of so "unexpected" immigrants.

10th MP: *We must take measures to avoid rationing.*

The financial recession of year 2008 created millions of jobless people. About <u>one percent</u> of them found better jobs pretty soon; these pals are affectionately called the Hals. (<u>H</u>appy <u>a</u>nd <u>l</u>ucky guy<u>s</u>)

Initially, both the experts and the lay folks referred to this recession as "the crisis". But now, six years later, due to its unexpected duration and enormity, it is called "The Great Recession"; and many of its victims are known as the Larrys. (**L**engthy **a**nd **r**udely **r**ationed gu**ys**)

What happened in 2008 was a financial rebalance and, the truth be told, people could see it coming. But people were in denial.

It seems that another kind of rebalance is approaching and, since there are so many Deniers, it is worth to mention this warning: *"When the time of environmental reckoning comes, we **all** will be Larrys."*

11th MP: ***We must abandon the growth bubble*** (exponential, long-term, sustained, recruitment**).**

Remember the fighter-jet parable: It can't climb indefinitely; sooner than later it will run out of airlift or fuel.

The time is ripe for Humanity to pay more attention to other phases of our mission: cruising altitude, enjoy the flight, descent, soft landing, rest, evaluation, planning, resupplying.

12th MP: ***We must embrace frugality.***

We shall not confuse frugality with poverty or pauperism. Frugality is the decision to live richly with fewer things; it empowers the human beings, it pleases God. Poverty is the decision to live richly with more things; it weakens the human beings, it displeases God. Pauperism is a fact, not a decision, and we all shall contribute to rescue the victims of such misfortune.

13th MP: ***We must reject those political-projects that exacerbate the overpopulation.***

Many politicians become anxious about their "legacy", and they will push whimsical pet projects without considering their costs.

Some of such projects can exacerbate the overpopulation, the damage to pristine areas, and the fiscal debt; such is the case of the Californian bullet-train. This dream of the current Governor has already lost most of the "promised" funding and the support within the voters; in spite of that, this Governor insists on fulfilling this "legacy"!

Californian voters are realizing that the bullet-train is going to be a financial parasite, a white elephant demanding perpetual subsidies.

Did you know that in Europe and Asia, even in their overpopulated areas, almost all the bullet-train routes are subsidized? Just a few of such routes are genuinely self-sustained!

14th MP: Mother Nature, Mother Earth, Ms. HaloHabitat.

These feminine characterizations, besides acknowledging women as the fountain of life and kindness, are a **Call to female solidarity:**

Ladies! Only you can appease Ms. HaloHabitat; only you can stop us the males from irreparably alienating Her.

15th MP: Ladies! **Do not count on us the males to lead the missions that uniquely you shall lead.**

You got to examine one of the most disappointing examples of <u>right mission ↔ inadequate leadership</u>: the task of attaining a Responsible Level of Human Population (**RLHP**) has been trusted to .....us? .....the males!?

Ladies! Take a panoramic look at Humanity's predominantly male leadership. Haven't you noticed that ---when it comes to **RLHP**--- we the males may have the best of intentions but .....we don't know what we are talking about? .....Don't trust us!!

Ladies! You must keep in mind that, in the spheres of selfishness and idiocy, we the males are far more selfish and idiotic than you. .....Don't go to those spheres!!

16th MP: Ladies! You have what it takes to preserve, protect and defend your children's and grandchildren's HaloHabitat:

Apply your powers! Rational, spiritual, educational, financial, social, feminine, decision, charms, the purse strings.

17th MP: **Humanity needs new ideas at the MACRO level of Philosophy, Religion and Economics.**

In other words, new contributions to the Master Plans.

Ladies, you know that your contributions to these universes have been nixed by us the arrogant males; but we still need you.

It is hard to admit this but, without you, we are lost!